PICTURE LEVEL
Book 4

MULTIPLE SKILLS
SERIES: Reading

Third Edition

Richard A. Boning

SRA McGraw-Hill

Columbus, Ohio

A Division of The McGraw·Hill Companies

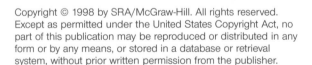

SRA/McGraw-Hill

A Division of The **McGraw·Hill** *Companies*

Send all inquiries to:
SRA/McGraw-Hill
250 Old Wilson Bridge Road
Suite 310
Worthington, Ohio 43085

ISBN 0-02-688401-1

3 4 5 6 7 8 9 SCG 02 01 00 99 98

PURPOSE

The *Multiple Skills Series* is a nonconsumable reading program designed to develop a cluster of key reading skills and to integrate these skills with each other and with the other language arts. *Multiple Skills* is also diagnostic, making it possible for you to identify specific types of reading skills that might be causing difficulty for individual students.

FOR WHOM

The twelve levels of the *Multiple Skills Series* are geared to students who comprehend on the pre-first- through ninth-grade reading levels.

- The Picture Level is for children who have not acquired a basic sight vocabulary.
- The Preparatory 1 Level is for children who have developed a limited basic sight vocabulary.
- The Preparatory 2 Level is for children who have a basic sight vocabulary but are not yet reading on the first-grade level.
- Books A through I are appropriate for students who can read on grade levels one through nine respectively. Because of their high interest level, the books may also be used effectively with students functioning at these levels of competence in other grades.

The **Multiple Skills Series Placement Tests** will help you determine the appropriate level for each student.

PLACEMENT TESTS

The Elementary Placement Test (for grades Pre-1 through 3) and the Midway Placement Tests (for grades 4–9) will help you place each student properly. The tests consist of representative units selected from the series. The test books contain two forms, X and Y. One form may be used for placement and the second as a posttest to measure progress. The tests are easy to administer and score. Blackline Masters are provided for worksheets and student performance profiles.

THE BOOKS

This third edition of the *Multiple Skills Series* maintains the quality and focus that have distinguished this program for over 25 years. The series includes four books at each level, Picture Level through Level I. Each book in the Picture Level through Level B contains 25 units. Each book in Level C through Level I contains 50 units. The units within each book increase in difficulty. The books within a level also increase in difficulty—Level A, Book 2 is slightly more difficult than Level A, Book 1, and so on. This gradual increase in difficulty permits students to advance from one book to the next and from one level to the next without frustration.

Each book contains an **About This Book** page, which explains the skills to the students and shows them how to approach reading the selections and questions. In the lowest levels, you should read About This Book to the children.

The questions that follow each unit are designed to develop specific reading skills. In the lowest levels, you should read the questions to the children.

In the Picture Level, the question pattern in each unit is
1. Title (main idea)
2. Picture clue
3. Picture clue

The **Language Activity Pages** (LAP) in each level consist of four parts: Exercising Your Skill, Expanding Your Skill, Exploring Language, and Expressing Yourself. These pages lead the students beyond the book through a broadening spiral of writing, speaking, and other individual and group language activities that apply, extend, and integrate the skills being developed. You may use all, some, or none of the activities in any LAP; however, some LAP activities depend on preceding ones. In the lowest levels, you should read the LAPs to the children.

In the Picture Level, each set of Language Activity Pages focuses on a particular skill developed through the book. The first and third LAPs focus on picture interpretation. The second and fourth LAPs focus on main ideas.

SESSIONS

The *Multiple Skills Series* is an individualized reading program that may be used with small groups or an entire class. Short sessions are the most effective. Use a short session every day or every other day, completing a few units in each session. Time allocated to the Language Activity Pages depends on the abilities of the individual students.

SCORING

Students should record their answers on the reproducible worksheets. The worksheets make scoring easier and provide uniform records of the children's work. Using worksheets also avoids consuming the books.

Because it is important for the students to know how they are progressing, you should score the units as soon as they've been completed. Then you can discuss the questions and activities with the students and encourage them to justify their responses. Many of the LAPs are open-ended and do not lend themselves to an objective score; for this reason, there are no answer keys for these pages.

The words and sentences in a story belong together. They all help to tell about one **main idea**. Listen to this story. Think about what it is mainly about.

Jon was planning a party. He made a list of friends to invite. He made a list of things to buy.

What do all of the sentences in the story tell about? Would "Jon Plans a Party" be a good namc for thc story? Figuring out what a story is mainly about is important in reading.

In reading we also need to remember the **facts**. The facts are the things the story tells. In the story above, what was the boy's name? What did he do? A good reader pays attention to the facts.

A story doesn't always have words. Sometimes a **picture** tells a story. When you look at a picture, you can figure out what it is mainly about. You can look carefully at the picture to remember what it shows. When you do this, you are a good reader.

In this book, you will look at pictures. After you look at a picture, choose a **title**, or name, that tells what the picture is mainly about. Then answer two questions about what the picture shows.

1. The best title is—

   (A) The Girl Is Flying

   (B) The Girl Is on a Rope

2. There are three—

   (A) girls

   (B) boys

3. The boys are—

   (A) standing

   (B) sitting

1. The best title is—

   (A) The Dog Is Running Away

   (B) The Dog Wants a Ride

2. You can see a—

   (A) car

   (B) truck

3. The dog is—

   (A) on the grass

   (B) by a tree

1. The best title is—

    (A) The Boys and Girls Are Sad

    (B) The Boys and Girls Are Singing

2. The boys and girls are in a—

    (A) school

    (B) house

3. You can see—

    (A) toys

    (B) books

1. The best title is—

    (A) Father Has a New Boat

    (B) Father Has a New Car

2. Father is—

    (A) in the car

    (B) *not* in the car

3. You can see a—

    (A) girl

    (B) boy

1. The best title is—

    (A) The Girl Is Painting

    (B) The Girl Is Reading

2. You can see—

    (A) the sun

    (B) a train

3. The goat is—

    (A) running

    (B) eating

1. The best title is—

   (A) The Girls Are Talking

   (B) The Girls Are Eating

2. The girls are in a—

   (A) car

   (B) tree

3. There are—

   (A) three girls

   (B) two girls

A. Exercising Your Skill

Look at the picture. What is the girl doing? Answer the questions in the story map.

Where is the girl?

_____

> The Girl Is Painting a Picture

What is she painting?

_____

B. Expanding Your Skill

Think about the words in the box. They tell things that are in the picture. One word does not belong. Tell the words that belong.

girl	paints	fence	dog	trees

C. Exploring Language

Tell what you see in the picture in Part A. Fill in the blanks.

The girl is ____ in a field. It is a nice day. The ____ is shining. The girl wears ____ to see better. The girl is painting a picture of a ____ . The goat is eating ____ .

D. Expressing Yourself

Do one of these things.

1. Make up a story about the girl. Tell why you think she likes to paint.

2. Tell three things that you like to do for fun. Tell why you like to do them.

1. The best title is—

   (A) Baby Can Read

   (B) Baby Can Walk

2. The baby has a—

   (A) book

   (B) toy

3. The baby is going to—

   (A) Father

   (B) Mother

1. The best title is—

    (A) The Girl Likes to Work

    (B) The Girl Is Going Fast

2. You can see—

    (A) trees

    (B) cars

3. The girl is going down a—

    (A) hill

    (B) road

1. The best title is—

   (A) The Boys Are Playing

   (B) The Boys Are Working

2. The boys have a—

   (A) pet

   (B) ball

3. The boys are by a—

   (A) boat

   (B) house

1. The best title is—

   (A) The Girl Goes to School

   (B) The Girl Has Pet Fish

2. The fish are—

   (A) falling

   (B) eating

3. You can see—

   (A) three fish

   (B) two fish

BIKE PATH

1. The best title is—

   (A) The Boys Like to Ride

   (B) The Boys Are on a Boat

2. There are—

   (A) two boys

   (B) four boys

3. You can see a—

   (A) bed

   (B) boat

1. The best title is—

   (A) At the Farm

   (B) At the Beach

2. You can see a—

   (A) boat

   (B) fish

3. One girl is—

   (A) walking

   (B) sitting

A. Exercising Your Skill

Think about the story below. Finish the story map. Make up a title for the story.

The boys are outside. They are playing basketball. They run and they jump. They try to get the ball in the basket. They try to take the ball away from each other. They like to play ball.

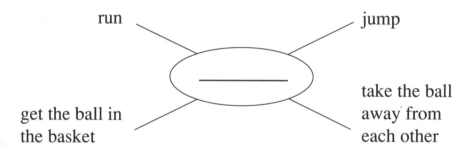

run   jump

—————

get the ball in   take the ball
the basket   away from
                       each other

B. Expanding Your Skill

Make up a title or heading that tells about the words in the box. Then try to add two things to the list.

soccer football baseball basketball

C. Exploring Language

Look at the picture in Unit 12. Tell about the picture. Use your own paper. Put your own words where there are blanks. Then give the story a title.

The girl and her mother are at the ____ . The mother sits on a ____ . Near the sleeping girl is a ____ . A ____ sits in the water.

D. Expressing Yourself

Do one of these things.

1. Make up a story about a day at the beach or the park. Give the story a title.

2. What sports do you like to play? Tell about two sports you like and why you like them.

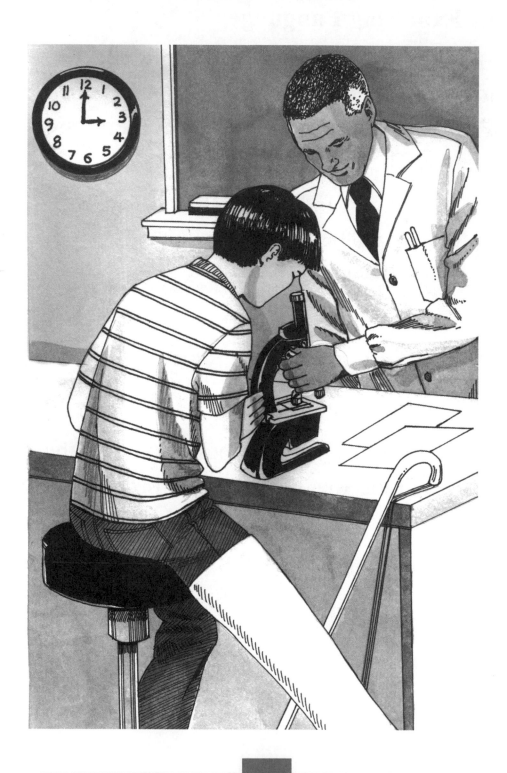

1. The best title is—

    (A) The Man Helps the Boy

    (B) The Boy Is Playing

2. The boy is—

    (A) standing

    (B) sitting

3. You can see a—

    (A) car

    (B) clock

1. The best title is—

    (A) The Girl Is Playing

    (B) Shopping with Mother

2. You can see a—

    (A) bike

    (B) girl

3. The girl has a—

    (A) bag

    (B) net

1. The best title is—

   (A) The Girl Wants to Read

   (B) The Girl Hears Something

2. The girl is in—

   (A) school

   (B) bed

3. You can see a—

   (A) book

   (B) TV

1. The best title is—

   (A) The Tree Is Falling

   (B) The Men Are Going

2. You can see a—

   (A) truck

   (B) bird

3. The men have a—

   (A) car

   (B) saw

1. The best title is—

   (A) The Girl Has Two Pets

   (B) The Girl Is Looking for the Cat

2. The cat is by a—

   (A) tree

   (B) bike

3. The girl has a—

   (A) coat

   (B) hat

1. The best title is—

   (A) The Girls Are on a Boat

   (B) The Girls Are at Home

2. One girl is—

   (A) jumping

   (B) sitting

3. You can see a—

   (A) boat

   (B) train

1. The best title is—

   (A) The Girls Are Having Fun

   (B) The Girls Want to Help

2. The girls are—

   (A) riding

   (B) wet

3. One girl has a—

   (A) fish

   (B) hat

A. Exercising Your Skill

Look at the picture. Then answer the questions.

1. What kinds of foods are in the store?
2. What does the woman want to buy?
3. What kind of fruit does the girl have?

B. Expanding Your Skill

Think about the picture in Part A. Tell which words below are foods you see in the picture.

grapes   tomatoes
bananas   celery
oranges   pears

C. Exploring Language

Pretend you are the person who sells food at the store. On your paper, use your own words where there are blanks.

I work in a grocery ___ in a big ____ . I sell fruits and I sell ___ . I love the colors of the foods I sell. I love the ___ tomatoes! I love the ___ grapes. Best of all, I love the ___ oranges!

D. Expressing Yourself

Do one of these things.

1. Play "What Food Am I?" Tell about a food. Do not name it. Ask your friends to name it.

2. Make up your own story about the food store. Draw a picture to go with your story.

1. The best title is—

   (A) The Man Likes to Go Fast

   (B) The Man Is Planting

2. The plant is by the—

   (A) lake

   (B) house

3. You can see a—

   (A) window

   (B) car

1. The best title is—

   (A) The Dog Is Running

   (B) The Dog Is Riding

2. The dog is going—

   (A) down a hill

   (B) up a hill

3. The men are—

   (A) jumping

   (B) looking

1. The best title is—

   (A) The Girl Is Helping

   (B) The Girl Is Playing

2. You can see the girl's—

   (A) mother

   (B) father

3. There is a lot of—

   (A) rain

   (B) snow

1. The best title is—

   (A) The Fire Is Out

   (B) The Man Makes a Fire

2. The man is—

   (A) big

   (B) little

3. You can see a—

   (A) bag

   (B) car

1. The best title is—

    (A) The Boy Gets a Toy Train

    (B) The Train Is Coming

2. One man has a—

    (A) bike

    (B) book

3. You can see a—

    (A) baby

    (B) cat

1. The best title is—

    (A) The Girl Is Talking

    (B) The Girl Is Riding

2. You can see—

    (A) one car

    (B) two cars

3. The man is in a—

    (A) house

    (B) car

A. Exercising Your Skill

The school bus pulled up to the red brick school. The children got off the bus. Their teachers were there to greet them. The school day was off to a good start!

Think about the story. Then finish the story map below. Give a title for the story.

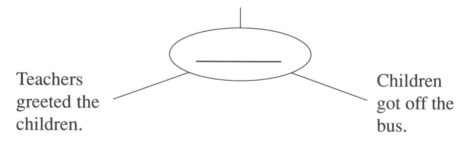

School bus pulled up to the red brick school.

Teachers greeted the children.

Children got off the bus.

B. Expanding Your Skill

Read or listen to the words in the box. Make up a title or heading that tells about the things in the box. Then add two more things to the list.

desks	chairs	teachers	students

C. Exploring Language

Finish the story. Fill in the blanks with your own words. Use your own paper.

The name of my school is ___ .
I am in ___ grade. My teacher's
name is ___ . The principal's
name is ___ . My favorite thing to
do is ___ .

Now give the story a title.

D. Expressing Yourself

Do one of these things.

1. Write or tell about your school day. Tell some things you like to do in school.

2. Make up a story about a school bus driver. Make up a funny story about one thing that happened on the bus.